Weight Watchers™

Low Point

Family meals

Over 60 recipes low in Points

SIMON & SCHUSTER
A VIACOM COMPANY

Cas Clarke

Published in Great Britain by Simon & Schuster UK Ltd, 2000.

A Viacom Company.

Copyright © 2000, Weight Watchers International, Inc.

First published 2000

Reprinted 2003

Simon & Schuster UK Ltd.

Africa House

64–78 Kingsway

London WC2B 6AH

Weight Watchers and *1, 2, 3 Success 2000* are Trademarks
of Weight Watchers International, Inc. and used under its
control by Weight Watchers (U.K.) Ltd.

Photography: Steve Baxter

Styling: Marian Price

Food preparation: Jane Stevenson

Design: Jane Humphrey

Typesetting: Stylize Digital Artwork

Printed and bound in China

Weight Watchers Publications Manager: Elizabeth Egan

Weight Watchers Publications Executive: Corrina Griffin

Weight Watchers Publications Assistant: Celia Whiston

A CIP catalogue record for this book is available
from the British Library

ISBN 0 743 23940 7

Pictured on the front cover: French-Style Sausage Casserole, page 20

Pictured on the back cover: Banana Muffins, page 52

contents

7

35

44

52

Whether you want to shed only a pound or two or many more, it is in your everyday meals that the key to success lies. By switching permanently to a lower-fat, healthy way of eating you can lose weight and, even more importantly, keep it off.

balanced
healthy
eating

A NEW WAY OF EATING

The Weight Watchers Programme is all about educating ourselves to realise that 'diet' isn't just a word that relates to a weight reduction programme – it relates to our normal, everyday eating. By changing your eating habits, you can successfully reach the weight that you want to be and stay there. We all need to realise that there are no right or wrong foods: there are foods that our bodies need to maintain health and well-being and foods of which we need to be careful how much we eat, as they are high in fat and calories and our bodies can only take so much of them before we start to put on weight.

FOOD TO SUIT YOUR WAY OF LIFE

This book is for those who want to follow this healthy way of eating, who lead busy lives and don't have lots of time to spend in the kitchen but do want to eat good, tasty meals every day – meals that you can cook easily whether you are eating alone, with a partner or with your family. Making sure that your everyday eating is low in Points lets you splash out on those special occasions – and still make it to your Goal!

**Kedgeree:
A tasty and
satisfying
supper dish
for the whole
family.**

These recipes are ideal for lunch or a light supper at the end of a long day. Some of these recipes are suitable when you want to make more of a meal but don't want to splash out on Points. Others such as the Roasted Tomatoes on Toast (page 16) and the recipe below make for a very special weekend breakfast.

KEDGEREE

POINTS

per recipe: $17^1/_2$ per serving: $4^1/_2$

Serves 4
Preparation & cooking time: 25 minutes
Calories per serving: 335
Freezing: not recommended

This makes a wonderful starter for six or an excellent weekend breakfast for four.

200 g (7 oz) long-grain rice
2 tablespoons medium curry powder
2 eggs
400 g (14 oz) smoked haddock fillets
300 ml (½ pint) fish or vegetable stock
garlic low-fat cooking spray
1 white onion, chopped
2 tablespoons chopped fresh parsley
2 tomatoes, each cut into 6 wedges
salt and pepper

1 Put the rice and curry powder in a pan and cover with water. Bring to the boil, cover and simmer for 10 minutes.

2 Meanwhile, hard-boil the eggs in simmering water for 8 minutes.

3 Place the haddock and stock in a large frying-pan, cover and cook for 6 minutes (until the fish flakes easily).

4 Using the low-fat cooking spray, cook the onion until just starting to brown.

5 When the fish is cooked, skin and flake the flesh.

6 When the eggs are cooked, plunge into cold water to cool and then remove the shells. Cut into wedges.

7 When the rice is cooked, drain if necessary and then stir in a tablespoon of chopped parsley, the cooked onion and cooked fish. Season with salt and pepper to taste.

8 Divide the kedgeree between four serving plates, garnish with wedges of egg and tomato and sprinkle with the remaining parsley. Serve immediately.

GREEN LENTIL SOUP

POINTS

per recipe: 9½   per serving: 2½

Ⓥ *Serves 4*

Preparation time: 5 minutes
Cooking time: 40 minutes
Calories per serving: 180
Freezing: not recommended

This is a basic soup that can be varied in many ways by adding herbs or spices. I particularly like it with a teaspoon of Worcestershire sauce.

200 g (7 oz) green lentils
1 onion, chopped finely
1 garlic clove, crushed
1 litre (1¾ pints) vegetable stock
1 tablespoon cornflour
salt and pepper

1 Put the lentils, onion, garlic and stock in a saucepan and bring to the boil.
2 Simmer for 40 minutes, until cooked.
3 Mix the cornflour with a little cold water and stir into the soup, to thicken it slightly.
4 Season well and serve.

VARIATION Make this into green lentil and lemon soup by adding the juice of half a lemon before serving.

ORIENTAL MACKEREL AND RICE

POINTS

per recipe: 4½   per serving: 4½

Serves 1

Preparation & cooking time: 15 minutes
Calories per serving: 305
Freezing: not recommended

Try this dish as a packed lunch and eat cold.

50 g (1¾ oz) long-grain rice
4 baby sweetcorn, each cut in half
1 tablespoon frozen peas
25 g (1 oz) cooked smoked mackerel fillets with crushed peppercorns
1 spring onion, sliced
½ teaspoon sesame seeds
soy sauce, to taste

1 Cook the rice in boiling water; drain.
2 Meanwhile, cook the sweetcorn and peas until tender, 3–4 minutes.
3 Remove the skin from the fish and flake the flesh.
4 When the rice and vegetables are cooked, mix together and place in a bowl. Top with the spring onion and fish. Sprinkle with the sesame seeds and season to taste with the soy sauce.

POTATO WEDGES WITH SPICY SALSA

POINTS

per recipe: 7   per serving: 3½

Ⓥ *Serves 2*

Preparation time: 5 minutes
Cooking time: 30 minutes
Calories per serving: 255
Freezing: not recommended

2 × 250 g (9 oz) potatoes, scrubbed and cut into 6 wedges
1 teaspoon paprika
2 teaspoons corn oil
salt
100 g (3½ oz) Salsa (see page 47), to serve

1 Preheat the oven to Gas Mark 7/ 220°C/425°F.
2 In a medium bowl, mix together the potato wedges, paprika and oil. Season with salt to taste.
3 Place on a non-stick baking tray and cook in the preheated oven for 30 minutes, turning once.
4 Serve with the spicy salsa for dipping.

VARIATION If you want to use Pace thick and chunky salsa sauce, this will increase the Points to 4 Points per serving.

Potato Wedges with Salsa: The ideal low-Point dip for these warm oven-baked potatoes.

TUNA CAKES WITH SPRING ONION SALSA

POINTS

per recipe: 8   per serving: 2

Serves 4
Preparation & cooking time: 30–35 minutes
Calories per serving: 135
Freezing: not recommended

This is a tasty treat for adults and children alike. Serve with a salad.

400 g (14 oz) potatoes, peeled and diced
185 g can tuna chunks in brine or spring water, drained and flaked roughly
salt and pepper

FOR THE SALSA

4 spring onions, sliced finely
5 cm (2 inches) cucumber, seeds removed and flesh diced finely
2 teaspoons lemon juice
1 teaspoon cooking oil

1 Boil or steam the potatoes for 15–20 minutes, until tender.
2 Whilst the potatoes are cooking, make the salsa by mixing together the spring onions, cucumber and 1 teaspoon of the lemon juice; leave to marinate.
3 When the potatoes are just cooked through, grate roughly, mix gently with the tuna and add the remaining lemon juice. Season well.
4 Heat the oil in a large, non-stick frying-pan.
5 Divide the potato mixture into eight and shape each portion into small rough cakes. Fry in the hot oil for 3 minutes on one side and then turn gently and cook for 2 minutes on the other side.
6 Serve the fish cakes with a helping of salsa.

Prawn Cocktail: A spicy pepper sauce gives this a delicious twist.

PRAWNS IN 'RED-HOT' COCKTAIL SAUCE

POINTS

per recipe: 5   per serving: 1

Serves 4
Preparation & cooking time: 5 minutes
Calories per serving: 75
Freezing: not recommended

Served with lettuce, this makes a perfect starter. With toast or slices of wholemeal bread it makes a very tasty lunch dish. Add the Points as necessary.

2 tablespoons white wine vinegar
2 tablespoons soy sauce
6 tablespoons tomato ketchup
½ teaspoon Tabasco or hot pepper sauce
1 small onion, grated
200 g (7 oz) peeled, cooked prawns, defrosted if frozen
lettuce leaves, to serve

1 Mix together the liquid ingredients and then add the onion and prawns; mix well.
2 In a serving glass or on a small plate, place some lettuce leaves and then top with the prawn mixture.

VARIATION Substitute the prawns with mixed seafood and adjust Points.

ROASTED TOMATO AND RED PEPPER SOUP, WITH GARLIC CROÛTES

POINTS

per recipe: 4   per serving: 1

V Serves 4

Preparation time: 10 minutes

Cooking time: 45 minutes

Calories per serving: 100

Freezing: recommended for the soup

---

6 tomatoes, skinned and halved

3 red peppers, de-seeded and cut into quarters

garlic low-fat cooking spray

4 thin slices (1 inch/2.5 cm) of French bread or 8 thin slices of French baguettine

450 ml (16 fl oz) vegetable stock

---

1 Preheat the oven to Gas Mark 6/ 200°C/400°F.

2 Place the tomatoes and red peppers on a baking tray and spray with the low-fat cooking spray.

3 Roast for 40 minutes.

4 Remove from oven. Liquidise.

5 Spray a clean baking tray with low-fat cooking spray and place the slices of French bread on it. Spray the bread with low-fat cooking spray and cook in the oven for 3–5 minutes, until starting to brown and crisp.

6 Meanwhile, mix together the liquidised vegetables and stock and warm through in a saucepan.

7 To serve, top the soup with a croûte or croûtes.

COOK'S NOTE To skin the tomatoes, place them in a small bowl, cover with boiling water for 30–60 seconds and then peel.

CURRY-STYLE MUSHROOMS ON TOAST

POINTS

per recipe: 3   per serving: 3

V Serves 1

Preparation & cooking time: 5 minutes

Calories per serving: 190

Freezing: not recommended

---

1 medium slice wholemeal bread

50 g (2 oz) mushrooms, halved or quartered, depending on size

2 tablespoons skimmed milk

30 g (1¼ oz) Pataks aubergine pickle

---

1 Toast the bread.

2 While the bread is toasting, heat together the other ingredients in a small pan until the mushrooms have softened slightly.

3 Serve the mushrooms and sauce on the toasted bread.

Roasted Tomato and Red Pepper Soup: Mini garlic toasts complement the sweetness of the roasted vegetables perfectly.

FETA-STUFFED PITTA

POINTS

per recipe: $4^{1}/_{2}$ per serving: $4^{1}/_{2}$

Ⓥ *if using vegetarian cheese*
Serves 1
Preparation & cooking time: 5 minutes
Calories per serving: 230
Freezing: not recommended

To vary this recipe, you can also add a little chopped garlic or mint sauce to the stuffing.

1 medium wholemeal pitta bread, warmed and halved

FOR THE STUFFING

25 g (1 oz) feta cheese, crumbled
few slices of red onion or spring onion
2 cherry tomatoes, or 1 standard tomato, halved or cut into wedges
few slices crispy lettuce (Iceberg or Little Gem)
1 teaspoon lemon juice
black pepper

1 Mix all the stuffing ingredients together before using to stuff the pitta bread.

PASTA IN CHEESY TOMATO AND BASIL SAUCE

POINTS

per recipe: $16^{1}/_{2}$ per serving: 4

Ⓥ *if using vegetarian cheese*
Serves 4
Preparation time: 15 minutes
Cooking time: 15 minutes
Calories per serving: 285
Freezing: not recommended

This super dish is very popular in our household and a good dish to make for lunch guests since it can be made in advance.

175 g (6 oz) pasta tubes
2 × 400 g cans of chopped tomatoes
2 teaspoons whole-grain mustard
2 garlic cloves, crushed
1 tablespoon chopped fresh basil
100 g (3½ oz) mozzarella cheese, grated

1 Preheat the oven to Gas Mark 4/ 180°C/350°F.
2 Cook the pasta in boiling water for 10 minutes.
3 Place the tomatoes, mustard and garlic in a pan and simmer for 10 minutes.
4 Add the basil and two-thirds of the mozzarella; stir until the cheese has melted.
5 Drain the pasta and mix with the sauce. Place in an ovenproof dish.
6 Sprinkle with the remaining cheese and bake in the preheated oven for 15 minutes.

Feta-Stuffed Pitta: The sunshine flavours of Greece in a bread pocket.

Brie and Courgette Soup: A creamy, filling and comforting soup.

TAGLIATELLE WITH PARMESAN

POINTS

per recipe: 18½   per serving: 6

Ⓥ *if using vegetarian cheese*

Serves 3

Preparation & cooking time: 10 minutes

Calories per serving: 380

Freezing: not recommended

A very quick and easy dish for when you are in a hurry.

250 g (9 oz) fresh tagliatelle

100 g (3½ oz) 95% fat-free extra-light low-fat soft cheese with onions and chives

3 tablespoons freshly grated parmesan cheese

black pepper

1 Cook the tagliatelle as directed on packet.

2 In a small saucepan, gently melt the soft cheese.

3 Drain the tagliatelle, toss all the ingredients together and season well with pepper. Serve immediately.

Tagliatelle with Parmesan: Ready in 10 minutes and perfect for the busy cook.

BRIE AND COURGETTE SOUP

POINTS

per recipe: 14   per serving: 3½

Ⓥ *if using vegetarian cheese*

Serves 4

Preparation time: 15 minutes

Cooking time: 15 minutes

Calories per serving: 170

Freezing: recommended

This soup can also be made by substituting mozzarella cheese for the Brie but it would then have 3 Points per serving.

200 g (7 oz) potatoes, peeled and diced

300 g (10½ oz) courgettes, halved lengthways and sliced

150 g (5½ oz) leek, halved lengthways and sliced

850 ml (1½ pints) vegetable stock

½ teaspoon dried thyme

135 g (5 oz) Brie cheese, rind removed, diced

black pepper

1 Put all ingredients, except the Brie, into a large saucepan.

2 Bring to the boil, cover and simmer for 12–15 minutes, until the vegetables are tender.

3 Add the Brie and stir until the cheese melts – do not overcook at this stage, this should only take 1–2 minutes.

4 Liquidise, season with black pepper and serve.

ROASTED TOMATOES ON TOAST

POINTS

per recipe: 1   per serving: 1

Ⓥ Serves 1

*Preparation time: 5 minutes +
20 minutes cooking
Calories per serving: 95
Freezing: not recommended*

You can substitute an equal amount of white-wine vinegar and ½ teaspoon light brown sugar for the balsamic vinegar.

100 g (3½ oz) cherry tomatoes
garlic low-fat cooking spray
½ teaspoon balsamic vinegar
sprinkling of dried thyme
1 medium slice of wholemeal bread
salt

1 Preheat the oven to Gas Mark 6/ 200°C/400°F.
2 Place the tomatoes on a baking tray, spray with the low-fat cooking spray and drizzle with the balsamic vinegar (or white-wine vinegar and sugar). Sprinkle with the thyme and salt and bake in the preheated oven for 20 minutes.

3 Toast the bread and serve the roasted tomatoes on this.

VARIATION Use the roasted tomatoes as a topping for baked potatoes or serve with pasta.

GLAZED GRILLED GRAPEFRUIT

POINTS

per recipe: 2   per serving: 1

Ⓥ Serves 2

*Preparation & cooking time: 10 minutes
Calories per serving: 60
Freezing: not recommended*

For a special occasion serve this as a starter and add a teaspoon of sherry to each grapefruit half before grilling. This will not add any Points.

1 grapefruit
1 tablespoon light brown sugar
½ teaspoon ground cinnamon

1 Preheat the grill for 5 minutes to high.
2 Cut the grapefruit in half with a sharp knife and loosen the segments.
3 Mix together the sugar and cinnamon and spoon this evenly over the grapefruit halves.
4 Stand the halves on a baking tray and grill for 4–5 minutes, until brown at the edges.
5 These can be served warm or be left to cool before serving.

GREEK PASTA

POINTS

per recipe: 10½   per serving: 5

Ⓥ *if using vegetarian cheese*
Serves 2
*Preparation & cooking time: 15 minutes
Calories per serving: 325
Freezing: not recommended*

Pasta is so versatile and this unusual dish is simply delicious.

120 g (4 oz) pasta
garlic low-fat cooking spray
100 g (3½ oz) courgettes, halved and sliced
100 g (3½ oz) tomatoes, skins and seeds removed (see Cook's note on page 11 for method), flesh diced
50 g (1¾ oz) feta cheese, crumbled
10 olives, sliced or halved

1 Cook the pasta in boiling water until just tender.
2 Meanwhile, using a non-stick frying-pan and the low-fat cooking spray, quickly brown the courgettes.
3 When the pasta is cooked, drain and mix with all the other ingredients. Serve immediately.

Greek Pasta: Something different for a quick, tasty supper.

**Minted Lamb
Casserole:
Perfect for
a warming
Saturday
supper or
Sunday lunch.**

family *favourites*

Here are some family favourites. Warming casseroles and bakes are always welcome during the colder months. Although some of these have longer cooking times, this brings out the flavours and the actual preparation time is low. Once the dish is in the oven you can forget about it and get on with something else. All these recipes are quick and easy to prepare – perfect for busy people.

MINTED LAMB CASSEROLE

POINTS	
per recipe: 14	per serving: 3½

Serves 4
Preparation time: 10 minutes
Cooking time: 1¾ hours
Calories per serving: 205
Freezing: recommended

Not only is this a super slimming recipe but family and friends will love it too!

400 g (14 oz) lean diced lamb
4 carrots, diced
1 leek, sliced
2 celery sticks, sliced
500 ml (18 fl oz) vegetable or lamb stock
20 g (¾ oz) gravy granules
1 tablespoon mint sauce

1 Preheat the oven to Gas Mark 3/ 170°C/325°F.

2 Put the lamb and vegetables into a casserole dish.

3 Using the stock and gravy granules, make a gravy and add the mint sauce to this. Pour into the casserole dish.

4 Cover and cook in the preheated oven for 1½ hours.

5 Uncover, stir and cook for a further 15 minutes before serving.

FRENCH-STYLE SAUSAGE CASSEROLE

POINTS

per recipe: 20   per serving: 5

Serves 4
Preparation time: 15 minutes
Cooking time: 1 hour
Calories per serving: 240
Freezing: recommended

A French favourite which is delicious served with mashed potatoes; just remember to count the Points.

454 g packet of extra-lean sausages
garlic low-fat cooking spray
1 onion, finely sliced
20 g (³/₄ oz) gravy granules
1 teaspoon white wine vinegar
1 dessertspoon whole-grain mustard
220 ml (8 fl oz) brown ale

1 Preheat the oven to Gas Mark 5/190°C/375°F.
2 Put the sausages on a baking tray and place in the preheated oven.
3 Using a non-stick pan and the low-fat cooking spray, gently fry the onion for 8–10 minutes, until starting to brown.
4 Meanwhile, using the gravy granules and boiling water, make 300 ml (½ pint) of gravy. To this, add the vinegar and mustard. Stir. Top up with beer.
5 Transfer the cooked onion to a casserole dish and top with the part-baked sausages. Add the gravy.
6 Reduce the oven temperature to Gas Mark 3/170°C/325°F. Cover the casserole and cook for ¾ hour.
7 Remove the cover, spoon the gravy over the sausages and cook for a further 15 minutes.

INDIAN SPICED LAMB

POINTS

per recipe: 31   per serving: 5

Serves 6
Preparation time: 10 minutes
Cooking time: 1³/₄ hours
Calories per serving: 360
Freezing: not recommended

This makes a wonderful Sunday lunch for a curry-loving family and is incredibly quick to put together if you have a food processor. Serve with some steamed broccoli.

½ leg of lamb (about 900 g/2 lb), extra trimmed
2 onions, grated or minced finely
4 teaspoons grated fresh root ginger
3 garlic cloves, minced
juice of ½ lemon (about 2 tablespoons)
150 g 0%-fat Greek yogurt
50 g (1³/₄ oz) ground almonds
250 g jar Tikka-flavoured Sharwoods Spice Blend

1 Preheat the oven to Gas Mark 4/180°C/350°F.
2 Mix all the ingredients together and spread all over the lamb.
3 Place the lamb on a rack and cook in the preheated oven for 1¾ hours.
4 If the lamb appears to be getting too black, cover with some foil.
5 Rest the lamb for about 10 minutes before carving into slices. With each slice, serve some of the crisp, spicy outside. Serve 3 slices for each portion.

**French-Style
Sausage
Casserole:
What could
be better than
low-Point
sausages and
mash?**

Tortilla-Topped Chicken Bake: Kids will love this unusual, fun-to-eat family dish.

TORTILLA-TOPPED CHICKEN BAKE

POINTS

per recipe: 24	per serving: 6

Serves 4
Preparation & cooking time: 25 minutes
Calories per serving: 330
Freezing: not recommended

An absolute winner with everyone.

garlic low-fat cooking spray
400 g (14 oz) boneless, skinless chicken thighs, cubed
295 g can of Mediterranean Tomato Soup
420 g can of Mixed Beans in Chilli Sauce
40 g (1½ oz) bag of tortilla chips
60 g (2 oz) half-fat mature Cheddar cheese, grated

1 Preheat the oven to Gas Mark 4/ 180°C/350°F.
2 Using a non-stick pan and the low-fat cooking spray, cook the chicken pieces for 5–8 minutes.
3 Add the soup and beans and mix well. Simmer for 5 minutes.
4 Place in a heatproof serving dish, sprinkle with the tortilla chips and cheese and bake for 10 minutes, until the cheese has just melted.

TUSCAN PORK

POINTS

per recipe: 11	per serving: 2½

Serves 4
Preparation time: 10 minutes
Cooking time: 35 minutes
Calories per serving: 175
Freezing: not recommended

300 g (10½ oz) passata
1 teaspoon Italian dried mixed herbs
1 small red pepper, de-seeded and chopped
garlic low-fat cooking spray
350 g (12 oz) extra lean pork steaks, and trimmed of all fat

50 g (1¾ oz) mozzarella cheese, grated
salt and pepper

1 Preheat the oven to Gas Mark 4/ 180°C/350°F.
2 In a saucepan, heat together the passata, herbs and red pepper.
3 Meanwhile, spray a non-stick pan and quickly fry the pork steaks for 2 minutes on each side to brown. Transfer to a shallow casserole dish.
4 Add the cheese to the passata sauce and stir until it melts. Season and pour over the pork.
5 Cover and cook in the preheated oven for 35 minutes.

Tuscan Pork: Add a little Italian flair to pork steaks.

ITALIAN CHICKEN CASSEROLE

POINTS

per recipe: 16	per serving: 4

Serves 4
Preparation time: 5 minutes
Cooking time: 1 hour
Calories per serving: 275
Freezing: recommended

Serve with vegetables or salad.

1 onion, grated
400 g can of chopped tomatoes
200 ml (7 fl oz) chicken stock
1 garlic clove, crushed
1 tablespoon dried mixed herbs
4 medium chicken thighs or 4 medium chicken drumsticks, skin removed
salt and pepper
20 stoned olives, halved, to serve

1 Preheat the oven to Gas Mark 4/ 180°C/350°F.
2 Place all the ingredients except the olives in a casserole dish. Mix well and season to taste.
3 Cover and cook in the preheated oven for 1 hour.
4 Just before serving, stir in the olives.

Italian Chicken Casserole: Yum!

VENISON CASEROLE

POINTS

per recipe: 11   per serving: 2½

Serves 4
Preparation time: 15 minutes
Cooking time: 2 hours
Calories per serving: 210
Freezing: recommended

Don't worry if the sauce flour seems lumpy when initially added to the casserole: keep stirring and it will dissolve.

350 g (12 oz) diced shoulder of venison
4 carrots, cut into matchsticks
1 onion, diced
100 g (3½ oz) button mushrooms, wiped
1 garlic clove, crushed
1 orange
250 ml (9 fl oz) red wine
1 tablespoon redcurrant jelly
1 tablespoon sauce flour

1 Preheat the oven to Gas Mark 4/ 180°C/350°F.
2 Put the venison and vegetables into a casserole dish with the garlic.
3 Cut two slices from the orange and cut each in half. Add to the casserole.
4 Juice the rest of the orange and add to the red wine. Make the liquid up to 400 ml (14 fl oz) with water.
5 Pour into the casserole and cover. Cook in the preheated oven for 1½ hours.
6 Add the redcurrant jelly and the sauce flour and stir well. Cook for a further 30 minutes before serving.

VARIATION Substitute 340 g (12 oz) diced lean braising steak for the venison and 200 g (8 oz) drained prunes in juice for the orange. This will be an extra 1½ Points per serving.

Venison Casserole: Venison and redcurrant jelly marry together beautifully in this dish.

TURKEY STROGANOFF

POINTS

per recipe: 12½   per serving: 3

Serves 4
Preparation & cooking time: 25 minutes
Calories per serving: 185
Freezing: not recommended

This is lovely served with rice and some fresh watercress. Don't forget to add the extra Points for the rice.

garlic low-fat cooking spray
450 g (1 lb) prepared turkey stir-fry strips
1 onion, chopped finely
200 g (7 oz) mushrooms, sliced
6 tablespoons half-fat crème fraîche
100 ml (3½ fl oz) skimmed milk
2 teaspoons Dijon mustard
salt and pepper
paprika, to garnish

1 Using a non-stick pan and the low-fat cooking spray, fry the turkey strips until browned.
2 Add the onion and mushrooms and continue to fry until cooked.
3 Add the rest of ingredients and stir well to form a sauce. Heat through and serve with a sprinkling of paprika on top to add some colour.

Beef Moussaka: A delicious, low-Point version of this traditional Greek dish.

BEEF, MUSHROOM AND POTATO MOUSSAKA

POINTS

per recipe: 34	per serving: 8½

Serves 4
Preparation time: 25 minutes
Cooking time: 35 minutes
Calories per serving: 485
Freezing: not recommended

It's worth parboiling the potatoes in this recipe since it drastically reduces the cooking time.

garlic low-fat cooking spray
500 g (1 lb 2 oz) extra-lean minced beef
2 garlic cloves, crushed
200 g (7 oz) mushrooms, chopped
400 g can chopped tomatoes
1 tablespoon tomato purée
600 g (1 lb 5 oz) potatoes, par-boiled for 5 minutes and sliced thinly
2 eggs, beaten
150 g tub of 0% fat Total yogurt (Greek yogurt)
100 g (3½ oz) half-fat Cheddar cheese
salt and pepper

1 Preheat the oven to Gas Mark 4/ 180°C/350°F.
2 Using a non-stick pan and low-fat cooking spray, brown the beef, garlic and mushrooms.
3 Add the tomatoes and tomato purée and simmer for 5 minutes. Season to taste.
4 Put half of this mixture in an ovenproof dish and cover with half of the precooked potatoes.
5 Repeat with the remaining meat and potatoes.
6 Beat the eggs, yogurt and cheese together and use this to top the moussaka.
7 Bake uncovered in the preheated oven for 35 minutes.

COOK'S NOTE You can jazz this recipe up so that it is suitable for a supper party by substituting wild mushrooms for the mushrooms in the recipe.

CRISP BEEF AND ✳ VEGETABLE PIE

POINTS

per recipe: 28½	per serving: 7

Serves 4
Preparation time: 25 minutes
Cooking time: 25 minutes
Calories per serving: 380
Freezing: not recommended

This produces very large helpings, ideal for cold winter evenings or those with large appetites!

low-fat cooking spray
500 g (1 lb 2 oz) extra-lean minced beef
1 onion, chopped finely
20 g (¾ oz) gravy granules
2 tablespoons horseradish sauce
500 g (1 lb 2 oz) mixture of prepared swede and carrots, diced and par-boiled until just tender, drained
400 g (14 oz) potato, par-boiled for 5 minutes and grated
2 teaspoons oil
salt and pepper

1 Preheat the oven to Gas Mark 5/ 190°C/375°F.
2 Using a non-stick pan and low-fat cooking spray, brown the mince and onion.
3 Make a gravy with the gravy granules and 300ml (½ pint) of boiling water. Stir in the horseradish sauce.
4 Mix together the beef, drained swede and carrot and horseradish gravy. Season.
5 Place in an ovenproof dish.
6 Top with the grated potato and brush with the oil. Season again.
7 Cook in the preheated oven, uncovered, until brown and crispy, about 25 minutes.

AUTUMN VEGETABLE GRATIN

POINTS

per recipe: 5¹/₂   per serving: 1¹/₂

V *if using vegetarian cheese*

Serves 4

Preparation time: 10 minutes

Cooking time: 30 minutes

Calories per serving: 95

Freezing: not recommended

---

250 g (9 oz) pumpkin, rind and seeds removed, flesh diced

---

350 g (12 oz) prepared root vegetables (not parsnips)

---

1 garlic clove, crushed

---

125 ml (4 fl oz) medium sherry

---

1 tablespoon cornflour

---

1 teaspoon dried mixed herbs

---

1 tablespoon freshly grated parmesan cheese

---

25 g (1 oz) fresh breadcrumbs

---

salt and pepper

---

1 Place all the pumpkin, root vegetables and garlic in a saucepan and cover with water. Bring to the boil and simmer until all are tender. This will take about 20 minutes, depending on your choice of root vegetables.

2 Preheat the grill to high.

3 Drain the vegetables, reserving the cooking water.

4 Place the vegetables in a gratin dish.

5 Add enough of the vegetable stock to the sherry to make 400 ml (14 fl oz).

6 Heat the sherry stock. Mix the cornflour with a little cold water and add it to the stock. Cook until slightly thickened.

7 Add the herbs and season well. Pour over the vegetables.

8 Sprinkle the parmesan and breadcrumbs over the top of the gratin.

9 Grill for about 10 minutes, until brown on top.

VARIATION You can replace the pumpkin with any other type of squash.

BOSTON BAKED BEANS

POINTS

per recipe: 23   per serving: 5¹/₂

Serves 4

Preparation time: 10 minutes

Cooking time: 2 hours

Calories per serving: 415

Freezing: not recommended

Begin this recipe the night before, by soaking the beans overnight.

---

200 g (7 oz) haricot beans, soaked overnight

---

1 onion, chopped finely

---

2 tablespoons brown sugar

---

2 tablespoons black treacle

---

1 tablespoon whole-grain mustard

---

454 g packet of low-fat sausages, each sausage cut into 3

---

1 Boil the beans for 10 minutes and then simmer for 30. Drain well.

2 Meanwhile, preheat the oven to Gas Mark 4/180°C/350°F.

3 Mix the beans and all the other ingredients together and put into a casserole dish with 100 ml (3½ fl oz) boiling water. Cover and cook in the oven for 1 hour.

4 Uncover and cook for 30 minutes more.

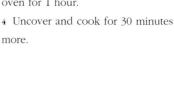

Autumn Vegetable Gratin: Root vegetables with garlic and cheese make divine comfort food.

Fish and Chip Pie: Imagine the delight of children (and grown-ups too!) when they see this pie topped with chips!

VEGETABLE PASTA BAKE

POINTS

per recipe: 18   per serving: 4½

Ⓥ *if using vegetarian cheese*

Serves 4

Preparation time: 20 minutes

Cooking time: 30 minutes

Calories per serving: 300

Freezing: not recommended

---

680 g jar of passata (sieved tomatoes)

low-fat cooking spray

300 g (10½ oz) carrots, diced

300 g (10½ oz) leeks, halved and sliced

500 g (1 lb 2 oz) courgettes, diced

2 garlic cloves, crushed

80 g (3 oz) mozzarella cheese, grated

8 fresh pasta sheets or cooked lasagne sheets

2 tablespoons half-fat crème fraîche

salt and pepper

1 Preheat the oven to Gas Mark 5/190°C/375°F.

2 Put a layer of passata in the bottom of an ovenproof dish.

3 Using a non-stick pan and low-fat cooking spray, stir-fry the carrots for 6–8 minutes. Then add the leeks and courgettes and cook for a further 2 minutes. The vegetables should be cooked but retain a little bite.

4 Meanwhile, in a small pan, heat the remaining passata, the garlic and half the cheese, until the cheese melts and you have a smooth sauce. Season to taste.

5 To assemble the bake, mix the tomato sauce with the vegetables. Put three pasta sheets in the bottom of the dish and top with half the vegetable mixture. Cover with three more pasta sheets and then the remaining vegetables. Place the last two sheets in the middle of your dish, cover with the crème fraîche and then sprinkle the remaining cheese all over the top of the dish (not just the pasta).

6 Bake in the preheated oven for 30 minutes.

VARIATIONS Use sliced mushrooms instead of courgettes. You can also use other types of pasta and just cook them for three-quarters of their cooking time before mixing in and baking.

FISH AND CHIP PIE

POINTS

per recipe: 14   per serving: 3½

Serves 4

Preparation time: 25 minutes

Cooking time: 30 minutes

Calories per serving: 230

Freezing: not recommended

This lovely fish pie has a light golden topping of chipped potatoes – delicious! This is one for all the family to enjoy.

---

370 g (13 oz) cod fillets, skinned

25 g (1 oz) sauce flour

300 ml (½ pint) skimmed milk

100 g (3½ oz) peas, cooked

salt and pepper

FOR THE TOPPING

400 g (14 oz) potato, par-boiled for 5 minutes and cut into matchstick shapes

2 teaspoons lemon juice

2 teaspoons oil

---

1 Preheat the oven to Gas Mark 6/200°C/400°F.

2 Poach or steam the fish for 8–10 minutes, until cooked.

3 Meanwhile, put the sauce flour and milk in a saucepan and bring to the boil, whilst stirring. When a sauce is formed, simmer very gently for 5 minutes.

4 Mix together the potato, lemon juice and oil for the topping.

5 To assemble the pie, mix together the flaked fish, peas and sauce. Season well. Place in the bottom of a shallow ovenproof dish. Top with the potatoes, season again and bake, uncovered, in the preheated oven, for 30 minutes, until the 'chips' are light brown and crisp.

COOK'S NOTE Sauce flour is now available in all major supermarkets.

ORIENTAL COD
WITH NOODLES

POINTS

per recipe: 15½   **per serving:** 4

Serves 4
Preparation & cooking time: 20 minutes
Calories per serving: 290
Freezing: not recommended

low-fat cooking spray

1 courgette, cut into matchstick shapes

*1 red pepper, cut into matchstick
shapes*

400 g can of chopped tomatoes

½ teaspoon Chinese five-spice powder

1 tablespoon soy sauce

*450 g (1 lb) cod fillet, skinned and cut
into bite-size chunks*

*200 g (7 oz) Chinese noodles, cooked
as directed on packet*

salt and pepper

1 Using a non-stick frying-pan and
the low-fat cooking spray, fry the
courgette and pepper for 3–4
minutes, until they start to soften.
2 Stir in the tomatoes, five-spice
powder, soy sauce and cod.
3 Cover and cook for 5 minutes,
until the fish starts to flake.
4 Stir into the drained noodles and
season before serving.

VARIATION You can omit the
noodles from this recipe and serve
with 200g (7 oz) rice (uncooked
weight). The Points will remain
the same. You can use any firm fish
for this recipe. Hake, salmon, tuna
and even swordfish are delicious
alternatives; just adjust the Points
as necessary.

SPANISH COD

POINTS

per recipe: 12½   **per serving:** 3

Serves 4
Preparation & cooking time: 25 minutes
Calories per serving: 185
Freezing: not recommended

Serve with rice (remember to add
the Points) and perhaps some salad.

*600 g (1 lb 5 oz) chunky cod fillets,
skinned*

250 ml (9 fl oz) white wine

250 ml (9 fl oz) vegetable or fish stock

*160 g jar of pimientos, drained and
chopped*

*150 g (5½ oz) sundried tomatoes,
rehydrated in water and chopped*

2 teaspoons Dijon mustard

2 teaspoons whole-grain mustard

*3 tablespoons finely chopped fresh
parsley*

1 Poach the fish in the wine
and stock, until cooked through
(about 12–15 minutes).
2 Remove the fish and keep warm.
Boil the cooking liquid until reduced
by half.
3 Add the rest of ingredients and
simmer for 2–3 minutes, to reduce
and thicken slightly.
4 Serve the fish with the sauce
spooned over.

COOK'S NOTE If you can't find
sundried tomatoes, cherry tomatoes
would be a good substitute. This
will reduce the Points per serving
by a ½. You can vary this recipe
by substituting any type of drained
antipasti (available in most major
supermarkets) for the pimientos, or
even by adding a little chopped red
pepper or mushroom which has been
quickly fried using a low-fat spray.

Oriental Cod with Noodles: Fish is so delicious with the flavours of the Orient.

**Thai Chicken
Stir-Fry: A taste
of Thailand,
in only 15
minutes.**

When everyone in the family seems to have a different schedule with varying working hours, after-school clubs and so on, family meals often have to be flexible. This may mean everyone eating at different times and that's when it's good to be able to reach for these quick recipes for one or two. They are as fast and as easy to prepare as many convenience foods but taste much better. The recipes can of course also be doubled or tripled for those times when more of the family can be assembled!

quick meals for one or two

THAI CHICKEN STIR-FRY

POINTS

per recipe: $2^{1}/_{2}$ per serving: $2^{1}/_{2}$

Serves 1
Preparation & cooking time: 15 minutes
Calories per serving: 195
Freezing: not recommended

A tasty, yet simple dish which can be put together quickly for a single supper.

low-fat cooking spray
1 medium boneless, skinless chicken breast, sliced very thinly
1 carrot, cut into matchstick shapes
2 spring onions, sliced
$^{1}/_{2}$ red pepper, de-seeded and thinly sliced
1 tablespoon soy sauce
$^{1}/_{4}$ teaspoon grated fresh ginger
$^{1}/_{2}$ teaspoon cornflour
4 tablespoons water

1 Using a non-stick pan and the low-fat cooking spray, stir-fry the chicken and vegetables for 5 minutes.
2 Mix together the rest of the ingredients and add to the pan.
3 Mix in well and cook for 2–3 minutes, stirring constantly.

COOK'S NOTE Add fresh coriander and chilli without adding any extra Points.

JAMAICAN CHICKEN

POINTS

per recipe: $4^{1}/_{2}$ per serving: $4^{1}/_{2}$

Serves 1
Preparation time: 5 minutes + 1 hour marinating
Cooking time: 15 minutes
Calories per serving: 240
Freezing: not recommended

This is a quick treat for those who like spicy food. Serve with a mixed salad (which is Points free!) and some boiled white rice, adding Points for the rice.

150 g (5$^{1}/_{2}$ oz) boneless, skinless chicken breast
85 g (3 oz) Tropic Isle Jamaican Chicken Marinade
salt and pepper

1 Season the chicken, spread the marinade over it, cover and leave to marinate for 1 hour.
2 Preheat the grill to medium.
3 Cook the chicken breast for 8 minutes on the first side. Turn and cook for 7 minutes on the second side. Serve at once.

Jamaican Chicken: This wonderfully spicy chicken is the most popular dish in Jamaica.

CHICKEN KEBABS WITH HERB AND GARLIC DIPPING SAUCE

POINTS

per recipe: 6   per serving: 3

Serves: 2

Preparation & cooking time: 15 minutes + 1 hour marinating

Calories per serving: 150

Freezing: not recommended

Fun to make and a delicious dinner for two. Serve with Spiced Carrot Salad (see page 48) and rice remembering to add the Points.

juice of ¹/₂ lime

2 teaspoons soft brown sugar

¹/₂ teaspoon paprika

150 g (5¹/₂ oz) boneless, skinless chicken breasts, cut into bite-sized pieces

FOR THE DIPPING SAUCE

60 g (2 oz) extra-light cream cheese with garlic and herbs

2 tablespoons skimmed milk

salt and pepper

1 In a small bowl, mix together the lime juice, sugar and paprika.

2 Stir in the chicken and marinate for 1 hour.

3 Soak two wooden kebab sticks in water (this stops them from burning during cooking). If you don't have wooden kebab sticks, use metal skewers, which obviously don't need soaking.

4 Preheat the grill to high.

5 Whisk together the cheese and skimmed milk, until you have a smooth sauce. Season to taste.

6 Thread 4–6 pieces of chicken on to each kebab stick.

7 Grill for 6–8 minutes, turning after 4 minutes. Serve with the dipping sauce.

VARIATION You can vary the dipping sauce by substituting other low-fat cheeses for the herb and garlic one used here.

CARAMELISED PORK AND APPLE

POINTS

per recipe: 9   per serving: 4¹/₂

Serves 2

Preparation & cooking time: 25 minutes

Calories per serving: 280

Freezing: not recommended

2 × 200 g (14 oz) pork chops, removed from the bone and all fat trimmed

¹/₂ teaspoon dried sage

2 thick rounds of apple, cut from a peeled, cored apple

1 tablespoon caster sugar

salt and pepper

1 Preheat the oven to Gas Mark 4/ 180°C/350°F.

2 Put the meat in a baking dish, sprinkle with sage and place the apple rings on top. Season to taste.

3 Cook for 15 minutes.

4 Mix the sugar with 2 teaspoons of water and spoon over the chops. Continue to cook for 10 minutes, until slightly caramelised.

VARIATION Ideal served with Potato Wedges (page 8) but don't forget to count the Points. Pork medallions work just as well as the chops in this recipe.

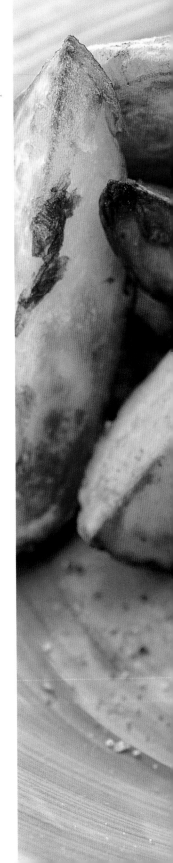

Caramelised Pork and Apple: The classic combination of pork with apples is delicious with a hint of caramel.

Sesame Beef
Stir-Fry: Quick
and easy but
incredibly good!

SESAME BEEF STIR-FRY

POINTS

per recipe: 5½   per serving: 2½

Serves 2
Preparation & cooking time: 15 minutes
Calories per serving: 245
Freezing: not recommended

This tasty recipe does have quite a long list of ingredients but it is still very easy to make.

low-fat cooking spray

150 g (5½ oz) thin-cut frying steak, sliced thinly

200 g (7 oz) carrot, cut into matchstick shapes

1 red pepper, de-seeded and sliced thinly

4 spring onions, split and cut into lengths

2 tablespoons soy sauce

2 tablespoons oyster sauce

2 tablespoons orange juice

1 tablespoon tomato ketchup

2 tablespoons water

1 teaspoon cornflour

1 tablespoon sesame seeds

1 Using a non-stick pan and the low-fat cooking spray, stir-fry the beef and vegetables for 3–4 minutes.
2 Mix together the rest of the ingredients.
3 Add to the pan, mix well and cook, stirring, for 3 minutes. Serve at once.

VARIATION Make this with chicken by substituting two medium chicken breasts for the frying steak. The Points per serving will be 3.

FILLET STEAK TOURNEDOS

POINTS

per recipe: 12   per serving: 6

Serves 2
Preparation & cooking time: 15 minutes
Calories per serving: 290
Freezing: not recommended

Serve with some steamed baby carrots and boiled potatoes, remembering to add the extra Points.

250 g (9 oz) fillet steak, halved vertically

garlic low-fat cooking spray

2 thin slices (1 inch/2.5 cm) French bread

FOR THE GARLIC BUTTER

1 tablespoon finely chopped fresh flat-leaf parsley

1 tablespoon half-fat butter

1 garlic clove, crushed

salt and pepper

1 Mash together the parsley, butter and garlic and season well. Form into a sausage shape and roll in cling film. Put in the freezer to chill.
2 Preheat the grill to high. Spray the steaks with low-fat cooking spray.
3 For medium steaks, grill the steaks for 5 minutes on each side.
4 Toast the bread.
5 When the steaks are cooked to your liking, place on the toast and top with slices of the chilled butter.

Fillet Steak Tournedos: The garlic butter makes this dish rather special.

HERBY LAMB

POINTS

per recipe: 2½   per serving: 2½

Serves 1
Preparation & cooking time: 15 minutes
Calories per serving: 245
Freezing: not recommended

This tasty treat can be served with
new potatoes and vegetables or a
salad, adding Points as necessary.

1 extra-lean medium lamb loin chop
garlic low-fat cooking spray
2 teaspoons each of finely chopped
fresh mint, parsley and chives
salt and pepper

1 Preheat the grill to high.
2 Spray one side of the lamb with
low-fat cooking spray and press half
of the herbs on. Season to taste.
3 Grill for 8 minutes.
4 Turn over and repeat. Serve
immediately.

VARIATION Another particularly
good combination of herbs is
coriander, mint and flat-leaf parsley.

SAUCED SOLE WITH GRAPES

POINTS

per recipe: 3½   per serving: 3½

Serves 1
Preparation & cooking time: 10 minutes
Calories per serving: 195
Freezing: not recommended

Although lemon sole has been used
here, plaice works just as well (add
1 Point per serving). Serve with
some peas and some boiled white
rice (remember to add the Points).

10 g (⅓ oz) sauce flour
100 ml (3½ fl oz) skimmed milk
bay leaf
200 g (7 oz) lemon sole, skinned
and filleted
6 grapes
wedge of lemon, to serve (optional)
salt and pepper

1 Preheat the grill to high.
2 In a small saucepan, mix together
the sauce flour and milk. Bring to
the boil, stirring. Add a bay leaf
and cook over a very low heat for
5 minutes.
3 Grill the sole fillets for 3–4 minutes.
4 Meanwhile, pour boiling water
over the grapes and then halve
(and de-seed them if necessary).
5 Place the cooked sole and grapes
on a serving plate, season the sauce,
remove the bay leaf and pour over
the fish. Serve with a lemon wedge,
if desired.

GLAZED SALMON STEAKS

POINTS

per recipe: 5   per serving: 5

Serves 1
Preparation & cooking time: 10 minutes
Calories per serving: 285
Freezing: not recommended

This produces a crispy skin which
is delicious. Serve with rice and a
refreshing green leafy salad. Add
the Points as necessary.

175 g (6 oz) salmon steak, skin on,
but cut in two and bone removed
¼ teaspoon mild chilli powder
¼ teaspoon soft brown sugar
¼ teaspoon white wine vinegar

1 Preheat the grill to medium.
2 Place the fish, skin side up, on
the rack. Mix together the other
ingredients and use to coat the skin.
3 Grill the fish for 6–8 minutes,
until the flesh is cooked and the
skin blackened and crisp. The skin
is good to eat too.

Glazed Salmon Steaks: Grilled salmon with a deliciously crispy skin.

Chick Pea Salad: A hearty, fresh-tasting salad full of satisfying flavour.

CHICK-PEA SALAD WITH HUMMOUS DRESSING

POINTS

per recipe: 8   per serving: 4

V *Serves 2*

Preparation time: 5 minutes

Calories per serving: 410

Freezing: not recommended

One of my favourite salad dishes, this is ideal for a buffet dish if made in larger quantities. It is delicious accompanied by crusty bread but don't forget to count the Points.

a few lettuce leaves, torn into bite-sized leaves

8 cm (3¼ inches) cucumber, sliced

½ carrot, grated

440 g can of chick-peas, drained

a few slices of red onion

2 tomatoes, cut into wedges

FOR THE DRESSING

100 g (3½ oz) reduced-fat hummous

4 teaspoons skimmed milk

1 Arrange the salad ingredients on two serving plates.

2 Whisk together the dressing ingredients and pour over the salads.

BAKED CHINESE TROUT

POINTS

per recipe: 4   per serving: 4

Serves 1

Preparation time: 5 minutes

Cooking time: 25 minutes

Calories per serving: 190

Freezing: not recommended

This tastes even better with some fennel seeds sprinkled inside the fish just before it is baked. Serve with some boiled noodles and remember to add the Points.

½ teaspoon sesame oil

2 teaspoons dark soy sauce

½ teaspoon Chinese five-spice powder

250 g (9 oz) trout, gutted and scaled and head removed if you wish

salt and pepper

1 Preheat the oven to Gas Mark 6/ 200°C/400°F.

2 Combine the oil, soy sauce and five-spice powder and use this to coat the fish. Season to taste.

3 Place the fish on a non-stick baking tray and roast in the preheated oven for 25 minutes, until the skin is crisp.

VARIATION With sea bass, the Points would be 4½ per serving.

VEGETABLE PAELLA

POINTS

per recipe: 6   per serving: 6

Ⓥ *if using vegetable stock*

Serves 1

Preparation & cooking time: 25 minutes

Calories per serving: 570

Freezing: not recommended

This is a very large serving for one person. If you served it with a salad it would be sufficient for two people.

---

125 g (4½ oz) basmati rice

350 ml (12 fl oz) vegetable or chicken stock

1 red pepper, de-seeded and diced

1 garlic clove, crushed

1 teaspoon paprika

200 g (7 oz) courgettes, diced

4 tomatoes, skinned, seeds removed and flesh chopped

salt and pepper

1 Place the rice, stock, pepper, garlic and paprika in a saucepan. Bring to the boil, then reduce the heat. Cover and simmer for 10 minutes.

2 Add the courgettes and tomatoes but do not stir. Cook for 3–5 minutes, until the liquid has been absorbed.

3 Season and stir the vegetables into the rice before serving.

VARIATION For a non-vegetarian paella, you could add one pre-cooked medium, skinless chicken breast, cubed. This will add 2½ Points.

DOMINICAN VEGETABLE CURRY

POINTS

per recipe: 8   per serving: 4

Ⓥ *Serves 2*

Preparation & cooking time: 25 minutes

Calories per serving: 275

Freezing: not recommended

This is ideal for those who like mild curries. Serve with some boiled white basmati rice and remember to count the Points.

---

100 g (3½ oz) potato, peeled and cut into large dice

200 g (7 oz) carrots, cut into large dice

100 g (3½ oz) cauliflower florets

100 g (3½oz) green beans, sliced

75 g (2¾ oz) peas

250 g jar Kerala flavoured Sharwoods Spice Blend

100 ml (3½ fl oz) water

salt and pepper

1 Cook the potato and carrots for 10 minutes in boiling water.

2 Add the cauliflower and green beans and continue to cook for 5 minutes.

3 Drain and return to the pan with the rest of the ingredients, stir well, bring to the boil, cover and simmer for 5 minutes.

VARIATION If you like curry to be hot, add some chopped red chilli when you add the spice blend.

simple side dishes

One of the things that people often miss when trying to change their eating habits is tasty side dishes to accompany their meals. But we don't have to serve our meals with vegetables or salads that are awash with butter or fattening dressings. There are lots of lovely things to do with vegetables to enhance their flavour whilst retaining their low-fat advantages.

THAI CUCUMBER SALAD

POINTS	
per recipe: 1	per serving: $^1/_2$

V *unless using fish sauce*
Serves 2
Preparation time: 5 minutes
Calories per serving: 45
Freezing: not recommended

This is a very easy salad to make and only a ½ Point per serving!

18 cm (7 inch) cucumber, halved, de-seeded and sliced thinly
2 spring onions, sliced
½ red chilli, de-seeded and sliced thinly

FOR THE DRESSING
1 tablespoon lime juice
2 tablespoons soy sauce
1 tablespoon water
2 teaspoons sugar

1 Mix together the dressing ingredients.
2 Combine with the salad and serve in a shallow dish.

COOK'S NOTE Add 1 tablespoon of fish sauce when making the dressing for a more authentic Thai flavour. Thai fish sauce is now widely available in supermarkets.

Thai Cucumber
Salad: Refreshing
and the perfect
companion for
Thai Chicken
Stir-Fry on
page 35.

Hot Coleslaw; Raita; Salsa: There are so many ways to serve vegetables with meals.

'HOT' COLESLAW

POINTS

per recipe: $4^1/_2$ per serving: 1

ⓥ Serves 4
Preparation time: 5 minutes
Calories per serving: 70
Freezing: not recommended

A quarter of a teaspoon of Tabasco sauce gives a nice 'kick' to the coleslaw – half a teaspoon will make it very hot!

250 g (9 oz) fresh coleslaw mix (white cabbage, carrot, onion)

FOR THE DRESSING

100 g ($3^1/_2$ oz) low-fat plain yogurt

50 g ($1^3/_4$ oz) low-fat mayonnaise

1 teaspoon white-wine vinegar

$^1/_4$–$^1/_2$ teaspoon Tabasco sauce

1 Mix the dressing ingredients together and use to coat the coleslaw mixture.

VARIATION This is delicious as a filling for a medium jacket potato, making the Points per serving $3^1/_2$.

RAITA

POINTS

per recipe: 1 per serving: $^1/_2$

ⓥ Serves 2
Preparation time: 5 minutes
Calories per serving: 45
Freezing: not recommended

An excellent accompaniment for curry dishes.

8 cm ($3^1/_4$ inches) cucumber, halved, de-seeded and diced finely

2 spring onions, chopped finely

2 teaspoons lemon juice

1 teaspoon mint sauce

125 g tub of low-fat plain yogurt

salt and pepper

1 Mix all ingredients together and serve.

VARIATION You can add some chopped fresh mint to this too.

SALSA

POINTS

per recipe: 0 per serving: 0

ⓥ Serves 2
Preparation time: 10 minutes
Calories per serving: 20
Freezing: not recommended

There are many ready-made salsas on sale, but home-made salsa is better since it has a fresher and tangier taste. If you make it for pre-dinner nibbles, your guests are sure to be impressed. It is excellent with Potato Wedges on page 8.

2 tomatoes, skinned, de-seeded and diced finely

5 cm (2 inch) cucumber, finely diced

3 spring onions, finely sliced

1 fat red chilli, de-seeded and sliced finely

1 teaspoon lime juice

1 Mix all ingredients together and serve.

'ROAST' POTATOES

POINTS

per recipe: 4½   per serving: 1

Ⓥ Serves 4

Preparation time: 15 minutes
Cooking time: 40 minutes
Calories per serving: 80
Freezing: not recommended

My children actually prefer these
to potatoes roasted in oil.

400 g (14 oz) potatoes, peeled and
cut into medium chunks
low-fat cooking spray
a pinch of paprika (optional)
salt and pepper

1 Preheat the oven to Gas Mark 5/
190°C/375°F.
2 Par-boil the potatoes for 6–8
minutes, until soft on the edges.
3 Drain the potatoes.
4 Spray a non-stick baking tray with
low-fat cooking spray and put in the
preheated oven for 1 minute.
5 Place the well drained potatoes on
the hot baking tray. Season with salt
and pepper, and paprika, if using.
6 Spray with oil and bake for 40
minutes, until crisp and beginning
to brown at the edges.

SPICED CARROT SALAD

POINTS

per recipe: 0   per serving: 0

Ⓥ Serves 2

Preparation time: 5 minutes
Calories per serving: 65
Freezing: not recommended

This is an excellent side dish for
curries or Chinese dishes.

200 g (7 oz) carrots, grated finely
1 tablespoon lemon juice
garlic low-fat cooking spray
2 teaspoons black mustard seeds
salt

1 Mix together the carrots and
lemon juice.
2 Spray a non-stick frying-pan with
low-fat cooking spray and heat it up.
3 Add the black mustard seeds and,
when they have 'popped', mix with
the carrot salad. Season well with
salt and serve.

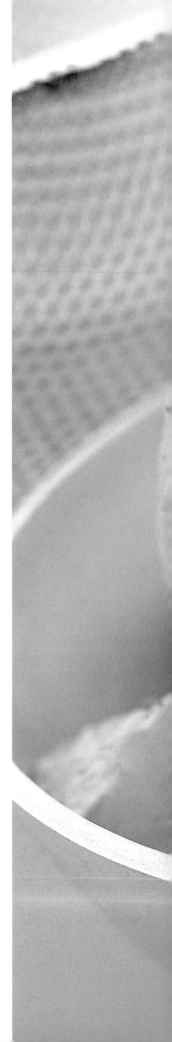

**Roast Potatoes:
A sprinkling of
paprika gives
these potatoes
a wonderful
golden colour.**

Rice and Vegetable Bake: This dish has a lovely mix of sweet and savoury flavours.

RICE AND VEGETABLE BAKE

POINTS

per recipe: 6   per serving: 3

v *if using vegetable stock*

Serves 2

Preparation time: 10 minutes

Cooking time: 45 minutes

Calories per serving: 250

Freezing: not recommended

An excellent all-in-one accompaniment to plain grilled or baked meat or fish dishes and it couldn't be easier to make.

120 g (4 oz) risotto rice
1 onion, chopped finely
200 g (7 oz) pumpkin, diced
550 ml (19 fl oz) vegetable or chicken stock
1 garlic clove, crushed
1 teaspoon paprika
1 teaspoon dried thyme
salt and pepper

1 Preheat the oven to Gas Mark 4/ 180°C/350°F.

2 Place all the ingredients in a shallow, ovenproof dish. Cook in the preheated oven for 20 minutes

3 Give the dish a good stir to turn all the rice grains over. Return to the oven for another 20–25 minutes or until the stock has been absorbed.

RICH VEGETABLE MEDLEY

POINTS

per recipe: 3½   per serving: 1

Serves 4

Preparation time: 15 minutes

Cooking: 30 minutes

Calories per serving: 85

Freezing: not recommended

v if you omit Worcestershire sauce and use vegetarian gravy granules (1 tablespoon is 1 Point). You could substitute red wine or brown ale for the stock for a slightly different flavour in this recipe and adjust the Points accordingly.

garlic low-fat cooking spray
1 onion, chopped finely
2 carrots, diced
1 red pepper, de-seeded and diced
200 g (7 oz) mushrooms, sliced
150 g (5½ oz) green beans, sliced
220 g can of chopped tomatoes
1 garlic clove, crushed
30 g (1¼ oz) gravy granules
250 ml (9 fl oz) vegetable stock
2 teaspoons whole-grain mustard
1 teaspoon Worcestershire sauce
salt and pepper

1 Preheat the oven to Gas Mark 6/ 200°C/400°F.

2 Using a non-stick pan and the low-fat cooking spray, quickly stir-fry the onion and carrots for a few minutes to soften and start to brown. Transfer all vegetables and garlic to a casserole dish.

3 Make a thick gravy with the gravy granules and 200 ml (7 fl oz) boiling water. Mix with the vegetable stock and add the mustard, Worcestershire sauce and seasonings to it. Pour into the casserole dish and mix well.

4 Cook in the preheated oven for 30 minutes.

Yes, you can have your cake and eat it – at least, when you make one of these! Although fruit is wonderful, there are times when we all feel like something more substantial. So here are some delicious treats to satisfy the urges we all get for something sweet which the whole family will enjoy.

Banana Muffins: Enjoy one with your tea or for breakfast with some fresh fruit.

BANANA MUFFINS

POINTS	
per recipe: 32	per muffin: 2½

ⓥ *if using free-range eggs*
Makes 12
Preparation time: 15 minutes
Cooking time: 25 minutes
Calories per muffin: 180
Freezing: recommended

These are gorgeous for breakfast served with honey or marmalade. Add ½ Point per heaped teaspoon.

250 g (9 oz) plain flour
1 teaspoon baking powder
1 teaspoon bicarbonate of soda
½ teaspoon salt
1 egg, beaten
5 tablespoons water
80 g (3 oz) soft brown sugar
3 medium well-ripened bananas, peeled and mashed to a purée
4 tablespoons corn oil

1 Preheat the oven to Gas Mark 5/ 190°C/375°F.
2 Put 12 paper cases in suitable muffin tins.
3 Sift together the flour, baking powder, bicarbonate of soda, and salt.
4 In another bowl, beat together the egg, water, sugar and bananas.
5 Add the corn oil to the wet ingredients and stir well.
6 Quickly combine the two sets of ingredients and mix just enough to combine – you should have a lumpy consistency.
7 Spoon the mixture into the paper cases and bake for 20–25 minutes, until firm and springy.
8 Cool on a rack.

& cakes
puddings

Plum Compote:
Plums are
delicious cooked
with red wine,
cinnamon and
vanilla.

PLUM COMPOTE

POINTS

per recipe: 4	per serving: 1

Ⓥ *Serves 4*
Preparation time: 5 minutes
Cooking time: 30 minutes
Calories per serving: 95
Freezing: not recommended

This is a dish that is ideal for either the family or entertaining.

8 ripe but firm plums
150 ml (¼ pint) red wine
1 cinnamon stick
few drops of vanilla extract
2 tablespoons soft brown sugar

1 Preheat the oven to Gas Mark 4/ 180°C/350°F.
2 Put the plums in an ovenproof dish and pour the wine over them.
3 Add the cinnamon stick and vanilla extract.
4 Sprinkle the sugar on top and bake, uncovered, in the preheated oven for 30 minutes.
5 Serve the plums with the flavoured wine spooned over them, discarding the cinnamon stick.

GLAZED SWEET PINEAPPLE

POINTS

per recipe: 4	per serving: 2

Ⓥ *Serves 2*
Preparation & cooking time: 10 minutes
Calories per serving: 115
Freezing: not recommended

This has to be tasted to be believed – healthy eating never used to be like this!

2 slices fresh pineapple
20 g (¾ oz) sugar
20 g (¾ oz) half-fat butter
1 tablespoon rum

1 Preheat the grill to high.
2 Place foil over the grill rack and place the pineapple slices on this. Sprinkle evenly with the sugar and grill for about 8 minutes, to caramelise.
3 Meanwhile, in a small pan, gently heat the butter and rum.
4 Serve the pineapple with the sauce spooned over.

VARIATION Substitute a small banana for each slice of fresh pineapple. The Points per serving will be 3.

GINGER PUDDINGS

Ⓥ if using free-range eggs

Serves 4

Preparation time: 10 minutes

Cooking time: 30 minutes

Calories per serving: 230

Freezing: recommended

These are delicious served with ice cream or a little golden syrup thinned with hot water. Adjust the Points accordingly.

80 g (3 oz) self-raising flour

½ teaspoon ground ginger

¼ teaspoon ground cinnamon

¼ teaspoon baking powder

¼ teaspoon bicarbonate of soda

1 egg, beaten

8 teaspoons corn oil

40 g (1½ oz) soft brown sugar

2 teaspoons golden syrup

75 ml (3 fl oz) warm water

1 Preheat the oven to Gas Mark 5/ 190°C/375°F. Have ready four 150 ml (¼ pint) pudding basins (tin, glass or foil).

2 Sift the dry ingredients into a bowl and then whisk in the rest of the ingredients.

3 Divide between the pudding basins and place on a baking tray.

4 Bake in the preheated oven for 25–30 minutes, until firm to the touch.

5 Cool in the basins for 5 minutes and then loosen with a knife and turn out.

BLACKBERRY FOOL

POINTS

per recipe: 5   per serving: 1

Ⓥ Serves 4

Preparation time: 10 minutes

+ 1 hour chilling

Calories per serving: 80

Freezing: not recommended

Blackberry Fool: Deliciously creamy and fruity and ideal for any occasion.

Those with a sweet tooth can add 2 teaspoons of caster sugar when they add the custard and yogurt; this will add ½ Point per serving.

400 g (14 oz) blackberries

200 g carton of low-fat ready-to-serve custard

100 g (3½ oz) 0% fat Greek yogurt

1 Purée the fruit roughly.

2 Mix in the custard and yogurt.

3 Spoon into a serving bowl or four individual bowls.

4 Chill for 1 hour before serving.

VARIATION You can substitute raspberries for the blackberries.

PURE INDULGENCE

POINTS

per recipe: 10   per serving: 5

Ⓥ Serves 2

Preparation time: 5 minutes

Calories per serving: 345

Freezing: not recommended

When you are really in a hurry but still want to enjoy a delicious dessert, this is ready in only 5 minutes and couldn't be easier!

200 ml (7 fl oz) Weight Watchers from Heinz Toffee Flavour Fudge Swirl Iced Dessert

200 ml (7 fl oz) Too Good to Be True 98% fat-free Frozen Dessert Chocolate

4 Askeys Café Curls

1 Using an ice-cream scoop, divide the desserts between two serving dishes and decorate with the café curls. Serve at once.

**Ginger Pudding:
If you love
ginger, you'll
make these
little puddings
again and again.**

**Baked Lemon
Pudding: No
one will ever
guess this
gorgeous
pudding is
low in Points!**

BAKED LEMON PUDDING

POINTS

per recipe: 15½   per serving: 4

Ⓥ *if using free-range eggs*
Serves 4
Preparation time: 10 minutes
Cooking time: 30 minutes
Calories per serving: 240
Freezing: not recommended

Another family favourite but without the usual Points.

40 g (1½ oz) half-fat butter

80 g (3 oz) light soft brown sugar

grated zest and juice of 1 lemon

2 eggs, separated

80 g (3 oz) self-raising flour, sifted

250 ml (9 fl oz) skimmed milk

1 Preheat the oven to Gas Mark 6/ 200°C/400°F.

2 Cream together the butter, sugar and lemon zest.

3 Beat the egg yolks and add them, with the flour. Stir well.

4 Add the milk and the juice of the lemon. Keep stirring until you have a smooth batter.

5 Whisk the egg whites stiffly and then very gently fold into the mixture.

6 Pour into a 1.2-litre (2-pint) pie dish and place this in a roasting tin with 3 cm (1¼ inches) of water in the bottom.

7 Cook in the preheated oven for 30 minutes, until firm and springy to the touch.

MINI PANCAKES

POINTS

per recipe: 9   per pancake: 1

Ⓥ *if using free-range eggs*
Makes 10 pancakes
Preparation time: 10 minutes
Calories per pancake: 55
Freezing: recommended (reheat in toaster)

These can be made for breakfast or as a dessert. Serve with melted jam, honey or maple syrup. They're also delicious sprinkled with lemon juice and caster sugar. Adjust the Points as necessary.

1 egg

125 g tub of low-fat plain yogurt

100 ml (3½ fl oz) skimmed milk

100 g (3½ oz) self-raising flour

½ teaspoon vanilla extract

a pinch of salt

1 teaspoon corn oil, for frying

1 Combine all your ingredients except the oil until you have a smooth batter.

2 Preheat a non-stick pan to which you have added the oil.

3 Drop spoonfuls of the batter into the pan and cook for 1–2 minutes on each side. Serve at once.

BAKED DOUGHNUTS

POINTS

per recipe: 12½   per mini doughnut: 1

v *if using free-range eggs*
Makes 12 mini doughnuts
Preparation & cooking time: 15 minutes
Calories per mini doughnut: 70
Freezing: recommended

You can now buy special baking sheets
for baking these mini doughnuts at
John Lewis or Lakeland. It's definitely
worth trying the recipe, as the
doughnuts make a delicious treat.

100 g (3½ oz) plain flour
1 teaspoon baking powder
1 egg, beaten
1 teaspoon corn oil
½ teaspoon vanilla extract
75 g (2¾ oz) caster sugar
4 tablespoons skimmed milk
½ teaspoon salt
low-fat cooking spray

TO SERVE

4 teaspoons caster sugar
½ teaspoon ground cinnamon

1 Preheat the oven to Gas Mark 3/
170°C/325°F.
2 Combine all the ingredients to
form a smooth batter.
3 Spray the baking sheet with low-
fat cooking spray. Almost fill each
doughnut hole, making sure you do
not overfill (or, when cooked, the
doughnuts will have no holes!)
4 Cook for 8–10 minutes, until risen
and firm to the touch.
5 On a small plate, mix together the
sugar and cinnamon for serving.
6 Remove the cooked doughnuts
from the tin. Dip the bottom of each
in the sugar and cinnamon mix and
leave to cool on a rack.

CARROT CAKE MUFFINS

POINTS

per recipe: 38   per muffin: 3

v *if using free-range eggs and*
vegetarian cheese
Makes 12
Preparation time: 10 minutes
Cooking time: 20–25 minutes
Calories per muffin: 210
Freezing: recommended (without icing)

These are delicious served fresh
with the icing or frozen on the same
day without icing and then served
warm as a breakfast treat with a
little blackberry jam. The Points per
serving without icing will be 2½.

250 g (9 oz) plain flour
1 teaspoon baking powder
1 teaspoon bicarbonate of soda
½ teaspoon salt
2 teaspoons ground cinnamon
1 egg, beaten
100 ml (3½ fl oz) water
1 tablespoon runny honey
100 g (3½ oz) soft brown sugar
300 g (10½ oz) carrot, grated finely
1 teaspoon vanilla extract
4 tablespoons corn oil

FOR THE ICING

*50 g (1¾ oz) Philadelphia light
cream cheese*
100 g (3½ oz) icing sugar
½ teaspoon orange juice

1 Preheat the oven to Gas Mark 5/
190°C/375°F.
2 Put 12 paper cases into suitable
muffin tins.
3 Sift together the flour, baking
powder, bicarbonate of soda, salt
and cinnamon.
4 In another bowl, beat together
the egg, water, honey, sugar, carrot
and vanilla.
5 Add the corn oil to the wet
ingredients and stir well.
6 Quickly combine the two sets of
ingredients and mix just enough to
combine – you should have a lumpy
consistency.
7 Spoon the mixture into the paper
cases and bake for 20–25 minutes,
until firm and springy.
8 Cool completely before icing.
9 To make the icing, just combine
the icing ingredients and spread
over the muffin tops.

Baked Doughnuts:
As delicious as
they look and
only 1 Point
each!

Strawberry Salad: This will really make summer strawberries something special.

COOKIES

POINTS

per recipe: 9   per cookie: 1

Ⓥ Makes 12

Preparation time: 10 minutes

Cooking time: 20 minutes

Calories per cookie: 45

Freezing: not recommended

Home-made cookies are always wonderful.

50 g (1¾ oz) half-fat butter

25 g (1 oz) caster sugar

75 g (2¾ oz) plain flour

¼ teaspoon vanilla or almond essence

1 Preheat the oven to Gas Mark 4/180°C/350°F.

2 Cream together the butter and sugar. Stir in the flour and essence to make a firm dough. (If you have the time, chill the dough for 30 minutes before continuing.)

3 Divide into 12 portions.

4 Take each portion, roll into a ball and then flatten and place on a non-stick baking tray.

5 Bake for 15–20 minutes, until pale golden. Leave to cool on the baking tray for 5 minutes and then transfer to a cooling rack.

MINCEMEAT SURPRISES

POINTS

per recipe: 30   per tart: 2

Ⓥ if using vegetarian mincemeat

Makes 15

Preparation time: 10 minutes

Cooking time: 20 minutes

Calories per tart: 100

Freezing: not recommended

A lovely winter dish to serve with low-fat custard (remember to add the Points) and to treat the kids with when they come home from school.

250 g (9 oz) ready-made puff pastry

150 g (5½ oz) luxury mincemeat

caster sugar, to serve

1 Preheat the oven to Gas Mark 6/200°C/400°F.

2 Roll half the pastry out to fit a small, non-stick baking tin.

3 Spread with the mincemeat.

4 Roll out the rest of the pastry and use to top the mincemeat. Sprinkle with a little icing sugar.

5 Bake in the preheated oven for 20 minutes.

6 Cool in the tin for 5 minutes and then cut into 12 portions.

STRAWBERRY SALAD

POINTS

per recipe: 3   per serving: 1

Ⓥ Serves 4

Preparation time: 5 minutes + 1 hour chilling

Calories per serving: 55

Freezing: not recommended

This may sound like an odd combination but it is very refreshing and makes a sophisticated party dessert.

400 g (14 oz) strawberries, hulled and sliced thinly

¼ teaspoon balsamic vinegar

2 tablespoons caster sugar

2 teaspoons finely chopped fresh mint

sprigs of mint, to decorate

1 Put the strawberries in a bowl and sprinkle with the other ingredients.

2 Chill for 1 hour.

3 Decorate with sprigs of mint and serve.